Contents

Introduction & Dorset Seafood Festival	4
The Bull's Fish Pie - The Bull Hotel	6
Pan-fried Mullet Fillets - By the Bay	8
Monkfish Peri Peri - Corkers Restaurant	10
Sand Sole - Crab House Café	12
Oven-baked Turbot - Fishy Fishy	14
Smoked Haddock Chowder - The Gaggle of Geese	16
Tea Smoked Razor Clam - The Greyhound	18
Local Sea Bass - Guildhall Tavern	20
Lyme Bay Mussels - Hive Beach Café	22
Red Gurnard - Hix Oyster & Fish House	24
Baked Brill - HV Restaurant	26
Jetty Crab Sundae - The Jetty	28
Pla Laad Prig - King & Thai	30
Cod Bourguignon - La Fosse at Cranborne	32
Lemon Sole - Quiddles	34
Braised Cuttlefish & Squid - Riverside Restaurant	36
Pan-fried Pollock - Shell Bay	38
Chuu Chee Hoi Shell - Thai Nakorn	40
Boscombe Bay Mackerel - Urban Reef	42
Roast Local Lobster - Vaughan's Bistro	44
Dorset Fishing Ports	46
Dorset Fisheries	48
Dorset Fish Species	50
Fishermen	52
Sustainability	54
Fishermen's Mission	58

This edition published in 2011 by:
Resort Marketing Ltd, 3 St Nicholas Street,
Weymouth, Dorset DT4 8AD
www.resortmarketing.co.uk

Recipes: Dorset restaurants

Editorial Contributions:
Dorset Coast Forum, Fishermen's Mission

Design & Layout:
Full Picture, www.fullpicture.co.uk

Photography:
© Dorset Coast Forum. Mark Simons

Food Photography: © Dorset Media Services

Printed by: Stephens & George, Merthyr Tydfil

ISBN: 978-0-9569454-0-2

Dorset Seafood Festival

Welcome to the Seafood Cookbook, published in association with the Dorset Seafood Festival. The annual festival promotes the Dorset seafood industry and sustainable fishing. The Royal National Mission to Deep Sea Fishermen is the festival's benefiting charity and £1.00 from each cookbook purchased will go to this worthy cause.

There can surely be no finer place to celebrate the rich harvest of the sea than Weymouth's charming 17th century harbourside. With fishing boats moored alongside and bars and pavement cafes lining the streets, the harbour is the perfect backdrop to the annual Dorset Seafood Festival, which takes place in July and is one of the highlights of the Dorset events' calendar.

Both sides of the harbour are taken over with stalls offering everything from delicious paella, sizzling scallops, barbecued king prawns, lobster salads, fish curries, seafood pasta and so much more. And if that's not enough then there are plenty of oysters and champagne to enjoy whilst soaking up the atmosphere.

The festival is organised by the Harbour Traders Association, which has been fortunate in securing Champagne Pommery as the title sponsor for 3 years from 2010 – 2012. Founded in 1836, Pommery is one of the most respected Houses with an impressive Domaine and underground cellars located in Reims in the heart of the Champagne region.

As well as the great seafood and champagne on offer there's also much to learn about fish and how to prepare it. Watch as experts show how easy it is to fillet a fish; see celebrity chefs create some amazing yet simple fish dishes; young chefs compete to become the 'Dorset Young Seafood MasterChef' of the year; and, of course, the stomach-turning Fishtucker Trials always attract a crowd of onlookers as brave volunteers sample some rather more unusual delicacies!

Since its inaugural event in 2008, The Dorset Seafood Festival has rapidly grown into one of the largest free seafood events in the UK. For more information please see www.dorsetseafood.co.uk

The Bull Hotel

The Bull Hotel
34 East Street
Bridport
DT6 3LF

Tel: 01308 422878

Pictured: Proprietors Richard and Nikki Cooper with Head Chef Marc Montgomery (centre)

www.thebullhotel.co.uk

Whether it's easy-going moules-frites (a Wednesday night institution in Bridport) laid-back weekend brunch, a lavish celebration meal, morning coffee or a Dorset cream tea, The Bull caters for every occasion with relaxed, rustic food in a busy, vibrant restaurant. Head Chef Marc Montgomery has created a menu with a strong emphasis on local seafood, meats and game to let the quality of the seasonal produce shine.

The Bull's Fish Pie

with Buttered Leeks and Gruyere Glaze

INGREDIENTS (Serves 4)

300g salmon & 300g hake, skinned, boned and cut into chunks

2 leeks, sliced

Knob of butter

100ml Noilly Prat vermouth

100ml white wine

Garlic, crushed

Thyme

500ml fish stock

250ml double cream

750g mashed potato

Gruyere cheese, grated

Seasoning

METHOD

Pre-heat oven to 180°c/350°f/gas 4. Melt butter in pan, add leeks, cover and cook until soft, stirring occasionally.

Meanwhile take a large pan and boil the fish stock rapidly until reduced by half.

In another pan boil vermouth, wine, garlic and thyme rapidly until reduced by half.

Add wine/vermouth broth to the reduced stock, add cream and again boil rapidly until reduced by half, season to taste (use the large pan as cream will bubble up).

Place fish in greased, ovenproof dish, add the cooked leeks then pour over hot sauce. Give it a gentle stir to ensure a good even mix of sauce, leeks and fish. Spread mashed potato on top and sprinkle with a generous layer of Gruyere.

Place in a pre-heated oven for 35 to 40 minutes until cooked through and the Gruyere has formed a glistening, golden glaze.

Top tip: Putting mashed potato on a fish pie can be awkward, resulting in the sauce spilling out over the top and the potato sinking. To avoid this ensure the potato is not too 'creamy'. Spoon the potato (desert spoon at a time) filling in around the edge of the dish first and working inwards to the centre. When filled carefully fork over sealing any holes. Either keep the forked, rough textured surface or smooth over with a palate knife before adding cheese.

By The Bay

By The Bay
Marine Parade
Lyme Regis
DT7 3JH

Tel: 01297 442668

Pictured: Chef Andy Hopkins

www.bythebay.co.uk

The lovely beach, harbour and bay that lap the doors of By the Bay Restaurant are the inspiration for many of Chef Andy Hopkins' delicious, coast-inspired dishes. He and his team produce mouth-watering fresh fish and seafood 'specials' every day alongside a comprehensive menu of delightful, traditional seaside fare with a modern, bistro twist. Using fresh produce, locally and sustainable sourced wherever possible, the restaurant is a favourite with local people and visitors alike.

Pan-fried Mullet Fillets

with Walnut & Parsley Pesto Dressing

INGREDIENTS (Serves 1)

Red mullet fillets

Plain flour

Vegetable oil

10g butter

Pinch each of sea salt & cracked black pepper

Lemon & parsley to garnish

Pesto Dressing

50g toasted walnuts

4 spring onions, chopped

1 clove garlic, crushed

Handful of fresh parsley, chopped

25ml extra virgin olive oil

METHOD

Place all the pesto ingredients into a food processor and blend until fairly smooth. Season generously.

Dust the fish fillets with flour and season.

Heat the oil in a skillet and pan fry the fish, skin side down until golden brown.

Flip the fish over and add a squeeze of lemon juice.

Sprinkle with chopped parsley.

The fish is cooked when it begins to separate under gentle pressure.

Transfer the cooked fillets to a serving plate and drizzle the pesto dressing over them.

Corkers Restaurant

**Corkers Restaurant
1 High Street
Poole
BH15 1AB**

Tel: 01202 681393

Pictured: Chef Steve Emery

www.corkers.co.uk

Why Peri Peri? This spicy tomato and sweet pepper sauce, complementary for meat and fish dishes, has been adapted from the Piri Piri sauce first experienced in Portugal many years ago. Chefs Steven Emery and Ken Clayton have created their own recipe around the original sauce and named it Peri Peri. Corkers' menus also include fresh fish and shellfish, grills and pasta, all offered in the elegant upstairs restaurant overlooking Poole Harbour.

Monkfish Peri Peri

INGREDIENTS (Serves 1)

175g monkfish tail (skinned and filleted)

140g fettuccine

1 tsp butter

Olive oil for frying

Sea salt & black pepper

Peri Peri Sauce

Half a medium onion finely diced

Half a red pepper sliced into strips

Half a yellow pepper sliced into strips

Half a bulb of fennel sliced into strips

1 tsp fennel seeds

1 x peri peri chilli

1 garlic clove

1 small tin of Italian tomatoes

1 tbsp olive oil

1 tbsp mango chutney

METHOD

Sweat fennel seeds, peri peri and garlic to flavour olive oil, add onion, peppers and fennel and cook until soft. Add tomatoes and cook until desired taste, flavour to sweeten with mango chutney. Finish with chopped fennel herb.

Season the monkfish lightly with sea salt and black pepper. Pan fry in a little olive oil and tsp of butter for about 5-6 mins, browning and sealing fish on all sides until just cooked.

Plunge fettuccine into boiling water and cook until al dente. Drain and place on the plate with the peri peri sauce and lay the monkfish on top.

Crab House Café

Ferrymans Way
Portland Road
Wyke Regis
DT4 9YU

Tel: 01305 788867

Pictured: Head Chef Adam Foster,
Proprietor/Chef Nigel Bloxham,
Apprentice Chef Shane Timbrell

www.crabhousecafe.co.uk

Dine in an idyllic ambience overlooking the
Portland coast and our own Oyster Farm in relaxed,
unpretentious surroundings, savour the finest flavours...
discover the hidden pearl of the South West, The Crab
House Cafe. Our menu changes once or twice a day,
depending on the fresh fish being landed. All of the
fish and our famous crabs are as fresh as can be, having
either been landed in Weymouth or Brixham. We pride
ourselves on using only local produce.

Sand Sole
with Crispy Oysters and Deep-fried Mackerel

INGREDIENTS (Serves 4)

For the Crispy Oysters

4 shucked oysters

6 large cabbage or purple sprouting leaves or broccoli

4 tbsp self-raising flour & 2 tbsp milk

½ tbsp salt & ½ tbsp sugar (mixed)

Oil for deep frying

Mackerel

4 small (Joey) mackerel or 2 medium

84g self-raising flour

170g cooked potatoes (firm)

2 tbsp tartare sauce

Dijon or English mustard

Sand Sole

4 small sand soles or small dabs (and flour for dusting)

Lobster shells and 20g lobster meat

250g clarified butter or ghee

Pinch sweet paprika

METHOD

Oysters

Poach the shucked oysters in their own juice; when firm lift out and drain on kitchen paper. Heat oil to 180°, finely shred cabbage or sprouting leaves to make 'seaweed'. Roll oysters in flour, dip in milk and return to flour, shake off excess and deep fry until crisp and golden, keep warm in oven. Deep fry shredded leaves until they stop sizzling. Season with salt and sugar mix, drain on kitchen paper then place on a tray in the oven to keep warm.

Mackerel

Spread the English or Dijon mustard on the flesh side of the fillets then dip in flour, then milk and return to the flour. Deep fry at 180° until crisp and golden. Keep warm in the oven. Dice the cooked potato and mix with the tartare sauce, squeeze lemon juice on to your liking and set aside.

Sand Soles

Take sand soles and trim frills, take tail and head off. Loosen skin where head was and grip with a cloth to release the skin then tear downwards.

Break up lobster shells and drizzle with oil, roast for 20 minutes in a moderate oven. Remove meat and set aside. Add the butter or ghee to the lobster shells and put in the oven until it melts, keep warm and melted. (Any leftover lobster shell butter will keep in the fridge for a month and will improve in flavour if you leave the shells in).

Put a pan on a medium heat, add a pinch of paprika and heat (do not burn), add butter or ghee. Dip both sides of trimmed soles in flour and fry in the butter until golden brown. When cooked put on a plate, you will see the flesh start to shrink from the bone, keep warm in the oven.

Chop lobster meat and add to the butter (you can use prawns instead, using the shells and the meat the same way). Warm through and spoon over the fish.

Place a small amount of potato tartare salad on the plate and place fried mackerel on top. Season crispy seaweed with sugar/salt mix to taste. On a plate place oyster shells onto the seaweed and put crispy oysters into the shells with a small piece of lemon. Serve and enjoy!

Fishy Fishy

Dolphin Quays
The Quay
Poole
BH15 1HH

Tel: 01202 680793

Pictured: Chef James Weare

www.fishyfishy.co.uk

Fishy Fishy Seafood Brasserie is owned by Dermot O'Leary and two of his closest friends, Paul Shovlin and James Ginzler. The restaurant has become popular both locally and with national food critics for its delicious local, fresh, seasonal fish and seafood and in summer 2011 launches its debut Fishy Fishy Cookbook. The relaxed, affordable restaurant has indoor and outdoor dining areas and overlooks the quay, with pretty views of Brownsea Island.

Oven-baked Turbot

with Braised Peas, Bacon and Baby Onions

INGREDIENTS (Serves 1)

1 x 500g tranche turbot

Olive oil for greasing

For the Peas

2 tablespoons olive oil

4 back bacon rashers

300g frozen peas

Juice of ½ lemon

Salt and freshly ground black pepper

250g baby silverskin onions

METHOD

A turbot can vary in size from 600g to 3-4kg. They are a slow-growing fish so should only be bought when 30cm or larger as they have then had a chance to spawn a couple of times.

Preheat the oven to 200°C/400°F/gas 6. Line a baking tray with greaseproof paper and lightly oil the surface.

A tranche is simply a cut from the spine out across the flat wing of the fish. Ask your fishmonger to do this, as the spine is quite thick and finding the correct spot to start the cut can be difficult.

Season the turbot and place in the oven for 20 minutes. Remove the turbot and look at the spine: the flesh should be just starting to go from pale to white, if it looks under-done then return to the oven for a few more minutes.

Heat the olive oil in a saucepan and fry the bacon rashers until golden brown. Add the peas and onions and cook

until tender, remove from the heat and squeeze over the lemon juice and season to taste.

Place a couple of handfuls of the braised peas in a bowl, lay the tranche of turbot on top and serve.

The Fishy Fishy Cook Book, published by New Holland, RRP £16.99

The Gaggle of Geese

**Buckland Newton
Dorchester
Dorset
DT2 7BS**

Tel: 01300 345249

Pictured: Chef/Proprietors:
Mark & Emily Hammick

www.thegaggle.co.uk

The Gaggle of Geese lies in the heart of the lovely village of Buckland Newton. Mark & Emily Hammick offer fabulous food, locally and seasonally sourced where possible, in a relaxed eclectic environment. With extensive grounds, lots of animals, an inviting log fire, local ales and ciders, a large selection of wines and amusing locals to converse with at the bar - what is there not to enjoy at The Gaggle!

Smoked Haddock & Smoked Mussel Chowder

INGREDIENTS (Serves 4)

For Poaching: 800g natural smoked haddock, filleted

1½ pints of milk

1 sprig each of thyme & sage

2 bay leaves

6 whole black peppercorns

2 parsley stalks

For the Sauce: 1 onion, 1 carrot & 1 stalk of celery

½ leek

50g of sweetcorn

2 medium potatoes, peeled

100g plain flour

1 tbls rapeseed or olive oil

50g butter

125ml white wine

50g parmesan & 50g mature cheddar, grated

½ tsp freshly chopped thyme

½ tsp freshly chopped parsley

½ tsp freshly chopped sage plus flowers

Garnish: 85g smoked mussels

METHOD

Preheat the oven to 180°C/gas 4. Bring the milk and poaching herbs to the boil. In a shallow tray place the smoked haddock and cover with the boiled milk and herbs. Cover with greaseproof paper and silver foil and place in the oven to poach for 20 minutes. Remove the fish and allow to cool.

Pass the milk through a fine sieve and reserve. Remove the skin and remaining bones from the haddock and flake into large chunks.

For the Sauce

Finely dice the onion, carrot, celery and leek and cube the potatoes into ¼ inch pieces. In a heavy based pan with a little oil, sweat the onion, carrot, celery and leeks until soft but without any colour. Add the potato cubes and cook for a further 2 minutes then add the butter and melt. Add flour and cook out for another 2 minutes. Slowly add the wine, stirring continuously to form a thick sauce. Then slowly add the poaching milk, stirring all the time, and

allow to thicken. Bring up to the simmer to thicken and then remove from the heat. Add the sweetcorn and stir in the parmesan and cheddar until dissolved.

Before serving add the flaked haddock to the sauce. Finish with the herbs and season to taste. Garnish with the smoked mussels and sage flowers.

Serve in a big bowl with a chunk of crusty bread.

Enjoy with a large glass of cold white wine.

The Greyhound

26 High Street
Sydling St Nicholas
Dorchester
DT2 9PD

Tel: 01300 341303

Pictured: Chef Deruke Tee

www.dorsetgreyhound.co.uk

The Greyhound at Sydling St Nicholas, deep in Thomas Hardy country, is Dorset's worst kept secret. Voted 'Dining Pub of the Year' twice in the last three years, the ancient pub, with six refurbished rooms and fragrant garden, has a wide reputation for great food and for its dynamic young team of managers and chefs. Hollywood loved the village so much it set the film 'Far From the Madding Crowd' in our churchyard.

Tea Smoked Razor Clam

and Brown Bread Chowder with Linguini Nero, Pancetta & Samphire Grass

INGREDIENTS (Serves 8)

700g razor clams
(substitute with Manila clams if razor are unavailable)

1 pint fish stock (preferably homemade)

200g brown bread

200g diced pancetta (or local substitute)

300g samphire grass
(available from most good fishmongers)

200g diced shallots

1 clove garlic, finely chopped

50ml Noilly Prat, (French vermouth available from most good off-licences)

300g squid ink linguini

350ml double cream

pomace oil (or light olive oil)

200g breakfast tea leaves

2 cinnamon sticks

4 bay leaves

4 star anise

METHOD

Wrap the tea leaves, cinnamon, bay leaves and star anise in a tin foil parcel. Spike the parcel well and place in a large, heavy bottomed pan, set over a very low heat. Place the clams in a metal colander over the saucepan and cover with spiked tin foil.

Gently smoke for approximately 30 minutes or until the clams open. Pick (remove) clams from shells (reserve 1 clam in-shell for garnishing).

In a separate pan, gently sweat the shallots, garlic and pancetta without colour. Once softened, deglaze with Noilly Prat, add the fish stock and cream and bring to the boil. Remove from the heat then add the bread and picked clams. Blend until frothed and smooth. Season with salt & pepper to taste.

Cook the linguine until al dente, add the samphire grass and drain almost immediately.

Lay the linguine on top of the samphire grass in a bowl, pour over the chowder and place the in-shell clam on top to garnish.

Top tip: Take care when seasoning as clams, samphire and pancetta retain salt.

Guildhall Tavern

Guildhall Tavern
Market Street
Poole
BH15 1NB

Tel: 01202 671717

Pictured: Chef/Proprietor
Frederic Seweryn

www.guildhalltavern.co.uk

"My name is Frederic Seweryn and I grew up on
the Cote d`Azur where I trained and honed my
cooking skills at famous fish restaurants in Antibes
and Juan les Pins.
My wife, Severine and myself, together with our
dedicated team put all our efforts into making the
Guildhall Tavern as successful as possible, and after
10 years our reward is to see both new and regular
customers eating with us."

Local Sea Bass

with Hand-picked Crab Meat & Lobster Sauce

INGREDIENTS (Serves 4)

4 whole sea bass (filleted)
at 600-800g each, skin on and scaled

1 lb of fresh crab meat
(50% brown 50% white)

1 lobster tail

1 carrot, 1 onion, 1 celery branch (all diced)

1 tbsp tomato puree

Fresh tarragon

200g samphire

2 tbls double cream

35ml Brandy

2 limes

2 garlic cloves

Butter

Olive oil, salt, cracked pepper

METHOD

Pre-heat the oven to 180°C/gas mark 4. Lay four of the fillets skin side down on a baking tray and remove all the bones. In a bowl, mix the crab meat together with lime juice, salt and pepper.

Cover the fillets with the crab stuffing and lay down the four remaining fillets (skin up) on the top of the crab meat.

Drizzle the fish with olive oil and cook in the oven for 15 minutes.

For the sauce: melt butter in a saucepan and sauté onion, carrot and celery until lightly browned, add lobster tail for 5 minutes (until pink) and flambé with brandy. Cover with water (one pint) add chopped tarragon and tomato puree and reduce to half the level.

Remove the lobster meat from its shell and blend it in the saucepan with the liquid.

Strain through a fine 'chinois' sieve and finish with cream. Adjust salt and pepper.

Place two fillets on each plate, surround with the sauce and top with sautéed samphire (just 20 seconds in the wok.)

Add a bit of personal touch with fresh herbs as seen in the photo.

Bon appétit!

Hive Beach Café

**Beach Road
Burton Bradstock
Bridport
DT6 4RF**

Tel: 01308 897070

Pictured: Chefs Barry George,
Tim Gibb and Tim Attrill
Proprietor, Steve Attrill

www.hivebeachcafe.co.uk

The Hive is an award-winning, family-run café
situated right on the beach and offering a vast
range of local foods. The fish counter is on view
as soon as you walk in and the chefs are at hand
to answer any questions. Breakfasts are legendary,
lunch is superb and as the sun goes down the Hive
mellows and melts romantically into supper. Please
check our website for opening times.

Lyme Bay Mussels

'Baked in a Bag' with Cider, Herbs and Cream

INGREDIENTS (Serves 1)

450g mussels

100ml cider

Splash of water

Tin foil, two sheets

BBQ

Herbs

1 sprig rosemary

1 sprig thyme

1 sprig parsley

2 bay leaves

METHOD

First prepare the mussels: pick off any showing beards (seaweed) and scrape off any barnacles. Any mussels found open which do not close when tapped, discard. Also discard any damaged ones. Thoroughly wash the mussels in clean, cold water to rinse off any grit.

Prepare the tin foil by laying two sheets over each other; place these sheets into a small oval dish to create a bowl shape. Next, place the clean mussels into the small oval foil dish; add the cider, a splash of water and the herbs. Wrap the sides of the foil up and over to create an enclosed 'pasty' or bag shape. Remove the bag from the dish and place straight onto the BBQ for five to ten minutes. The best way to tell if the mussels are cooked is to check that they have opened. Any that do not open, discard and do not eat.

Best served with a group of friends, a cool glass of wine or cider and crusty granary bread for dipping.

Why have we chosen this recipe?
We have chosen this dish as we feel this is a great one to cook with friends; it's simple, quick and tastes great. Health-wise, mussels are amazing; they are high in Omega 3 fish oils, high in Vitamin B12, rich in protein, zinc, Iron and selenium.
Sustainability? Farmed mussels are eco-friendly and sustainable and, unlike most other farmed fish, they require no chemicals and very little human intervention.

Hix Oyster & Fish House

**Hix Oyster & Fish House
Cobb Road
Lyme Regis
DT7 3JP**

Tel: 01297 446910

Pictured: Proprietor Mark Hix
Photographer Jason Lowe

www.hixoysterandfishhouse.co.uk

Hix Oyster & Fish House overlooks Lyme Regis harbour and boasts panoramic views across the Jurassic coast. We serve the best seafood we can find and do as little to it as possible so that you enjoy the real flavour of great British ingredients. The kitchen is run by head chef Phil Eagle and his team. Our daily changing menu features delights such as whole cooked Dorset Crab, whole grilled Lemon Sole and Monkfish Cheek curry.

Red Gurnard

with Sea Spinach, Steamed Cockles and Brown Shrimps

INGREDIENTS (Serves 4)

250–300g fresh cockles

2 red gurnard, each about 800g–1kg, scaled and filleted

2 shallots, peeled and finely chopped

50ml white wine

1 tablespoon chopped parsley

salt and freshly ground black pepper

100g butter

60g cooked brown shrimps, peeled or whole

A couple of handfuls of sea spinach, trimmed of any thick stalks and well washed

METHOD

To clean the cockles properly, leave them under cold running water for about 15 minutes, agitating them every so often to get rid of any sand. Check over the gurnard fillets for pin bones, removing any you find with tweezers.

Put the shallots in a pan with the white wine and bring to the boil. Add the cockles and parsley, season lightly and cover with a tight-fitting lid. Cook over a high heat for 2–3 minutes, shaking the pan a few times, until the cockles open, then stir in a good knob of butter and the brown shrimps. Discard any cockles that don't open.

While the cockles are steaming, melt 50g of the butter in a non-stick or well-seasoned heavy-based frying pan. Season the gurnard fillets and fry them skin side down over a medium heat for 3 minutes. Lower the heat, turn the fillets and cook for about 2 minutes on the flesh side.

At the same time, blanch the sea spinach in boiling salted water for 2–3 minutes, then drain well. Toss

in a pan over a low heat with a generous knob of butter and re-season if necessary.

Pile the sea spinach onto warm plates, lay the gurnard fillets on top and spoon over the cockles, shrimps and cooking liquor to serve.

British Seasonal Food by Mark Hix, Published by Quadrille, £25

25

HV Restaurant

**Thistle Hotel
The Quay
Poole
BH15 1HD**

Tel: 01202 666800

Pictured: Chef Gary Newman

www.thistlehotels.com

The restaurant offers stunning, panoramic views over Poole Harbour and provides British classics and seasonal seafood, most of which is sourced from Seafresh, a Hamworthy-based company. Guests can relax outside on the Marina Terrace for drinks or in the relaxed surroundings of the restaurant bar on the first floor.

Baked Brill

in Red Wine with Mash and Butternut Slabs

INGREDIENTS (Serves 1)

185g brill fillet (skin off)

150ml red wine

180g cold diced butter

200ml fish stock

50ml double cream

Clarified butter (for sealing brill)

200g chive mashed potato

180g butternut squash
(cut into squares and char grilled until half cooked)

Salt & pepper

26

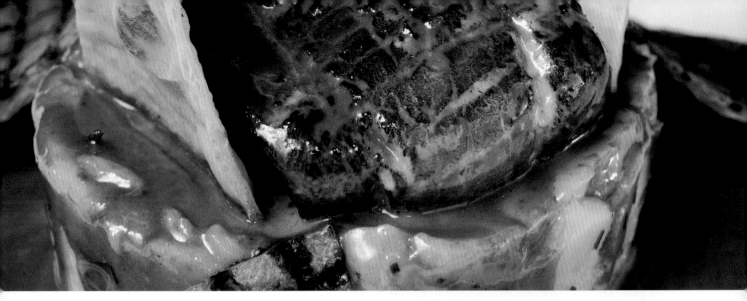

METHOD

Heat clarified butter in pan and seal brill on all sides, place on an ovenproof tray and leave to rest.

Deglaze pan with red wine and reduce by two thirds then add fish stock and reduce until nearly all gone. Add cream and reduce again by 50%; start adding the cold butter a little at a time, shake pan back and forth gently to monte au beurre sauce and it should thicken. Leave to one side to keep warm.

Preheat oven to 180°C/gas mark 4.

Place brill in a baking tray, cover with foil and cook for approximately 6-8 minutes. Also finish cooking the butternut squash in the oven until cooked.

Place hot mash in ring mould on plate then put the brill on top. Spoon warmed red wine and butter sauce around the fish adding a little over the fish. Place on butternut squash and serve.

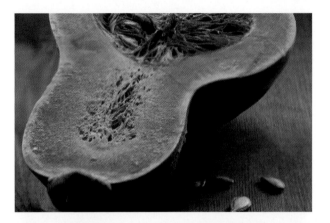

The Jetty

The Jetty
Christchurch Harbour
95 Mudeford
BH23 3NT

Tel: 01202 400950

Pictured: Chef Alex Aitken

www.thejetty.co.uk

The Jetty restaurant, bar and grill is set right on the water's edge looking across to Mudeford Quay. It's a terrific place to take in the breathtaking views and to choose something delicious off the menu. Fantastic fish is landed daily on the Quay and local producers drop off seasonal ingredients - it's these local flavours that Michelin starred chef, Alex Aitken and his team want to share and celebrate with the community.

Jetty Crab Sundae

INGREDIENTS (Serves 4 - 6)

250g fresh white crab meat
(preferably local Dorset brown crab)

50g brown crab meat

1 lemon (juice only)

1 tbsp of chopped chives

150ml mayonnaise

salt and pepper to taste

1 baby gem or cos lettuce

6 thin slices of dry cured smoked streaky bacon
(Denhay in Dorset produces great bacon)

For the Avocado Guacamole

2 ripe avocados, peeled and chopped

1 red chilli, de-seeded and finely chopped

2 tomatoes, peeled, de-seeded & chopped

2 limes, juice only

1 finely chopped shallot

1 small fresh garlic clove, crushed and finely chopped

METHOD

Mix the brown crab meat with the lemon juice, add the mayonnaise, fold in the white crab meat and chives. Check seasoning and store in fridge.

Use fresh, firm lettuce and roughly chop or tear into bite size pieces. Wash, put into iced water then drain, preferably using a salad spinner. Store in fridge.

Avocado Guacamole

Peel and de-stone the avocados then chop into chunks. Squeeze over the lime juice then smash together to create a paste, leaving some chunks of avocado. Add the chopped chilli, garlic, shallot and tomato. Check seasoning and add a little coriander if liked.

Crispy Bacon

Lay a sheet of parchment paper onto a baking sheet and lay on the strips of bacon without touching each other. Cover with another sheet of parchment paper and top

with a second baking sheet. Bake in a hot oven (180°C) for 10 minutes or until crisp and brown. The baking sheet should keep the bacon flat, although you may have to weigh it down.

Using glasses or bowls, layer up the sundaes. Start with the crunchy lettuce, then the guacamole then the crab mayonnaise. To finish, use the smoked bacon like a wafer. Add your own extra garnishes such as a wedge of lemon or quail's egg.

The King & Thai

The King & Thai
35-37 Great Western Rd
Dorchester
DT1 1UF

Tel: 01305 250270

Pictured: Chef Thep and
Proprietor/ Chef Somjit Thoumnok

www.thekingandthai.co

"Following 12 years work in the kitchens of a five star hotel in Pattaya, I moved to Europe to work in Paris then moved to the UK, initially employed as Head Chef, eventually becoming restaurant manager. The King and Thai is a contemporary restaurant providing a calm, relaxing atmosphere where, with Thep, our specialist chef, we serve authentic Thai cooking prepared with the finest quality, fresh, free range ingredients and spices." *Somjit Thoumnok*

Pla Laad Prig

Pan Fried Black Bream topped with a
Red Chilli and Garlic Sauce

INGREDIENTS (Serves 2)

Black Bream 400g to 600g - south coast May to Sep. (alternative: Gilt Head Bream farm grown)

Fish to be descaled, gutted and filleted. (A whole fish will serve 2 persons)

1 tbsp sunflower oil, reserve some for frying the fish

2 tbsp chopped fresh coriander for the paste and to garnish

3-6 finely chopped red chillies to suit your taste

1 small red onion peeled and finely chopped

3 cloves fresh garlic chopped

1 tbsp brown sugar

2 tbsp tamarind paste mixed with 4 tbsp warm water

3 tbsp Thai fish sauce

100ml fish stock, preferably homemade

Salt and pepper to taste

METHOD

First make the sauce by putting the coriander, chilli and garlic in a pestle and mortar and crush to a rough paste. Put a little of the oil in a frying pan and gently cook the onion until translucent then add the rough chilli paste and mix through, stirring for 2-3 minutes.

Add the tamarind paste, Thai fish sauce, fish stock and brown sugar and cook through for 3-4 minutes or until the sugar has dissolved. Taste for seasoning and then set aside but keep warm.

In a separate frying pan coat the base of the pan with the sunflower oil and put over a moderate heat. Place the fish fillets in the pan and cook for 2 minutes on each side.

Serve the fish on a plate and pour the warm sauce over the top. Garnish with fresh coriander.

La Fosse at Cranborne

**London House
The Square
Cranborne
BH21 5PR**

Tel: 01725 517604

Pictured: Chef/Proprietor
Mark Hartstone

www.la-fosse.com

La Fosse provides quality accommodation for dinner, bed and breakfast. We have six comfortable bedrooms and offer a friendly, efficient service, all set in the idyllic rural Dorset countryside. Relax in comfortable armchairs by the log fire, enjoy a glass of wine in the bar and choose from the fresh local, seasonal produce on the menu. It's the perfect base for exploring Dorset, the New Forest, the coast and neighbouring counties.

Cod Bourguignon

Our recipe is a twist on Mark Hartstone's 2006 National Seafood Challenge winning recipe

INGREDIENTS (Serves 4)

4 x 120g cod fillets

1ltr red wine

200ml port

½ltr demiglace

1ltr fish stock

200ml white wine fish sauce

250g butter

4 Maris Piper potatoes

Thyme, flat leaf parsley, bay leaves

Garnish

120g Pig Orchard onions (baby onions)

120g Cranborne pork lardons

120g Dorset Down mushrooms

120g Sopley broad beans

120g Alderholt asparagus

METHOD

Reduce wine by half, keep half to poach fish, add half to other stocks infusing thyme and bay, reduce till desired consistency, stir butter into sauce and season to finish.

Boil and puree potatoes, finish with fish sauce and butter, pass through a sieve.

Blanch green vegetables whilst sautéing other garnish.

Poach cod very slowly in red wine port reduction until firm to the touch.

This dish illustrates the La Fosse at Cranborne ethos of using fantastic local ingredients cooked with care and international inspiration. So where possible, use local ingredients from your area.

Quiddles

The Esplanade
Chesil Cove
Portland
DT5 1LN

Tel: 01305 820651

Pictured: Chef Adam Saint

See Quiddles Facebook page

Quiddles is a friendly and informal cafe sitting on the sea wall at Chesil Cove, Portland overlooking Lyme Bay. Specialising in seafood, which is caught and supplied by its owners, two local fishermen. Quiddles is famed for its alfresco Thursday night seafood paella (weather permitting). Paella parties can also be booked on the rooftop terrace or arranged at your own home. Open daily for breakfast and lunch. Evening meals served Friday and Saturday.

Lemon Sole

with Portland Crab and Smoked Salmon

INGREDIENTS (Serves 2)

Lemon sole, filleted

250g smoked salmon

125g Portland crab meat

200g samphire grass

Juice of ½ grapefruit

Juice of 2 limes

75g butter

75ml white wine

Sea salt

Rocket to garnish

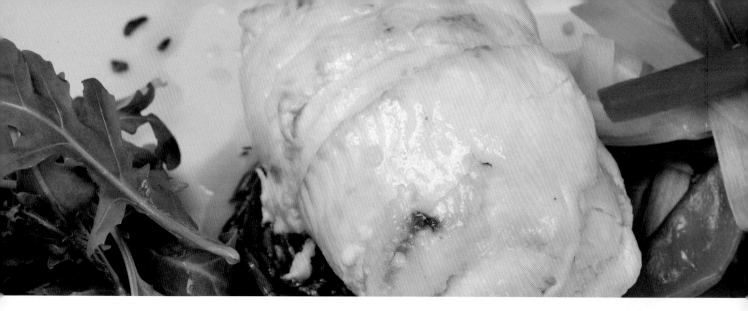

METHOD

Lay the sole fillets on a board then cover with smoked salmon topped with mixed crab meat. Gently roll together then wrap in cling film and put in the fridge to chill for 30 minutes.

Juice the limes and grapefruit and put to one side ready for the sauce.

Remove cling film and place the lemon sole onto a tray adding half the butter and the wine to the tray, sprinkle the fish lightly with sea salt and place under a moderate grill for 10 - 12 minutes until the fish is firm to touch.

Whilst the fish is cooking add the rest of the butter to a pan and pan fry the samphire grass. For the sauce, place the juice in a small pan and reduce to form a light syrup, adding a small amount of sugar.

Finally arrange the samphire on a plate and gently place the lemon sole on top. Spoon over the warm dressing and garnish with rocket leaves.

Riverside Restaurant

West Bay
Bridport
Dorset
DT6 4EZ

Tel: 01308 422011

Pictured: Assistant Manager &
Chef Nick Larcombe

www.thefishrestaurant-westbay.co.uk

Set in the heart of West Bay, on the bank of the River Brit, is the long established Riverside Restaurant. Famed for its seafood and loved for its relaxed and informal ambiance, its great emphasis is on local produce from the coast and countryside, delicious homemade desserts and extensive wine list. Although seafood is our speciality there are always meat and vegetarian options available.

Braised Cuttlefish and Squid

INGREDIENTS (Serves 4-6)

2 large cuttlefish, cleaned

2 large squid, cleaned

1 large onion, diced

2 cloves of garlic, crushed

1kg fresh tomatoes, skinned, deseeded and chopped

1 lemon, zested into 5 strips and juiced

1 orange, zested into 5 strips

2 fresh bay leaves

4 tbsp good olive oil

175ml red wine

Serve with fragrant rice and bread

METHOD

Slice squid and cuttlefish into thin strips and stir fry until slightly brown.

Remove from pan and set aside.

Heat half the oil in a medium size pan and sweat down the onion until soft.

Add in the garlic and tomatoes and bring to the simmer. Cook until the sauce is pulp-like.

Add the squid and cuttlefish to the tomato pan with the juices, bay leaves, orange and lemon zests.

Add the lemon juice and red wine and adjust for seasoning (salt and pepper).

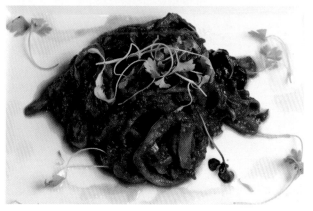

Bring back to the simmer, cooking until the fish is soft and tender – allow 1½ to 2 hours, stirring occasionally. Add a little water if the sauce looks a little too thick. Adjust seasoning and serve hot with fragrant rice and bread.

Shell Bay

Shell Bay
Seafood Restaurant
Ferry Road, Studland
BH19 3BA

Tel: 01929 450363

Pictured: Chef Dan Small

www.shellbay.net

Shell Bay Seafood Restaurant nestles on the edge of the Isle of Purbeck and overlooks stunning Brownsea Island, the waters of Poole Harbour and Sandbanks. Focusing on sustainable, locally-sourced seafood, direct from our own fishermen, the menu is fresh and totally innovative. Local oysters, succulent scallops, squeaky fresh bream and sea bass are just some of the menu favourites. With views of spectacular sunsets, Shell Bay is a place like no other.

Pan-fried Pollock

With Wilted Spring Greens, Dorset Cider, Mussels and Bacon Cream

INGREDIENTS (Serves 4)

4 x 8oz pollock portions

1 spring green cabbage

40 Poole mussels

100g dry cured smoked bacon

Sprig thyme

2 cloves garlic diced

White of 1 leek diced

1 stick of celery diced

1 banana shallot diced

200ml cider

100g butter

500ml double cream

Olive oil

Sea salt & pepper

METHOD

Roughly slice spring greens, careful to remove thick stems. Wash and dry. Place in heavily salted boiling water for 1 minute then into iced water. When cold drain and pat dry.

Place a heavy bottomed saucepan on the stove, wait until very hot and add mussels, cider, garlic, leeks, shallots, celery, thyme and butter. Cover with a lid and steam until mussels are open, add cream. Discard any mussels that do not open.

At the same time sauté diced bacon in pan until brown, add the mussels.

Add 2 spoonfuls of olive oil and a knob of butter to a pan over a medium heat. Season the pollock with sea salt and ground white pepper. Place in pan and leave until nearly cooked. Flip over, add a squeeze of lemon, remove pollock from pan and throw in the spring greens, sauté until warm.

Place the greens in the middle of a bowl and spoon over mussel broth, placing the pollock on top.

Thai Nakorn

Thai Nakorn
34 High West Street
Dorchester
DT1 1UP

Tel: 01305 756088

Pictured: Chef Wicha Kidhen

www.thai-nakorn.com

At Thai Nakorn our fresh, local ingredients are quickly cooked to preserve their nutrients and delicate flavours. Authentic Thai recipes are cooked by our highly experienced Thai chef/owner using traditional herbs and spices to create unmistakable Thai flavours. If you are looking for an alternative lunch meal, we offer our express lunch.
We are a fully licensed and air conditioned restaurant with a spacious and comfortable dining area.

Chuu Chee Hoi Shell

Dry Red Curry of Scallops

INGREDIENTS (Serves 1)

5 Lyme Bay King Scallops

2 tbsp fish sauce

½ cup of coconut milk

¼ cup of stock

3 tbsp of red curry paste

Pinch of sugar

Oil for frying

5 Kaffir lime leaves, finely shredded

Red chillies, finely sliced

Boiled broccoli

METHOD

Remove scallops from shells and wash.

Heat the oil in the pan. When the pan is heated, add scallops then turn. When just cooked, remove and rest in a warm place.

Pour some oil in then add red curry paste and fry over medium heat until fragrant. Season with sugar and fish sauce then add coconut milk. Continue to simmer, moistening with some stock. Check seasoning; it should be salty, hot, rich and slightly sweet.

Place the scallops and broccoli on the plate in the scallop shells then cover with curry sauce and garnish with lime leaves and red chillies.

Urban Reef

**The Overstrand
Undercliff Drive
Boscombe
BH5 1BN**

Tel: 01202 443960

Pictured: Chef Nigel Popperwell

www.urbanreef.com

International Design Award winning 'Urban Reef' is a funky and informal bar, café, deli and restaurant, located right on the beach in Boscombe. Opened in 2009, the venue's unique location offers panoramic views over Boscombe bay from its stunning first floor restaurant and promenade terrace. Owner of Urban Reef, Mark Cribb, is passionate about fresh local produce and simple but exceptional cooking, whilst always conscious of the environment and sustainability.

Boscombe Bay Mackerel

with Pepper Salsa

INGREDIENTS (Serves 2)

Two to three fresh Boscombe Bay mackerel (per person)

For the salsa

½ red pepper

½ yellow pepper

½ red onion

½ chopped mango

1 lemon

30g chopped English parsley or coriander

Dash of olive oil

Pinch of salt and pepper

For the side

Brioche bread

Side salad of rocket with some parmesan shavings and balsamic vinegar

METHOD

Cut the peppers and onion in a fine chop, place them into a pan and add the chopped mango.

Squeeze the juice from the lemon over the peppers, onion and mango then add the chopped herbs. Lightly cook for three minutes with a little olive oil. Add a pinch of salt and pepper to taste.

While the salsa is heating up, place the Boscombe Bay mackerel into a frying pan with a little olive oil. Cook the mackerel for two minutes on each side.

As the mackerel is cooking, lightly toast the brioche.

To finish, put the toasted brioche onto a couple of large plates, placing the mackerel on top. Spoon some salsa over each piece of fish then dress the plate with some olive oil. For the rocket salad, mix with olive oil, drizzle some balsamic vinegar on top and add the parmesan shavings.

To ensure the mackerel used for this recipe is sustainable, Nigel purchases the fish from a fishing boat named 'Déjà Vu' which fishes right outside Urban Reef, in the bay. This is a great dish to eat outside on a sunny day in the garden with a glass of chilled rosé wine; you'll feel like you're on a Mediterranean holiday! Enjoy it.

The culinary team at Urban Reef headed by exec chef 'Nigel Popperwell' are passionate about using the best local produce they can possibly find, sourcing ingredients from Dorset, Hampshire and the West Country.

Vaughan's Bistro

**Vaughan's Bistro
7 Custom House Quay
Weymouth
DT4 8BE**

Tel: 01305 769004

Pictured: Chef Mark Vaughan

www.vaughansbistro.co.uk

Vaughan's Bistro is situated right on Weymouth's harbourside and is perfectly placed for access to the freshest local fish. Around 90% of the fish used in the restaurant is bought locally, with lobsters arriving straight from the boats as they are unloaded on the quayside. Chef/proprietor Mark also sources meat and produce locally, and as Vaughan's only serves food that is in season the best of ingredients are assured all year round.

Roast Local Lobster

With Vaughan's Café de Paris Butter

INGREDIENTS (Serves 2)

2 local lobsters

For the Café de Paris Butter

1kg butter

60g tomato ketchup

25g each of Dijon mustard & capers (in brine)

125g shallots, finely chopped

50g each of fresh curly parsley & fresh chives

5g each of dried marjoram, dried dill & thyme

10 leaves fresh, French tarragon

5g fresh rosemary

1 garlic clove, squashed then chopped very finely

8 anchovy fillets (rinsed)

1 tbsp each of good brandy & Madeira wine

1 tsp Worcestershire sauce

½ tsp sweet paprika & ½tsp curry powder

Pinch cayenne

8 white peppercorns

Juice 1 lemon & zest of ½ lemon, zest ¼ orange

12g salt

METHOD

Café de Paris Butter

Mix all ingredients with the exception of the butter in a glass bowl and leave to marinate for 24 hours in a warm part of the kitchen (a slight fermentation occurs). Purée the mixture in a blender. Whip the butter and mix with the purée. Form into a log then cover and store in the fridge. You can also freeze it and cut off slices as you need them. The butter tastes even better when allowed to 'mature' for a couple of days.

Lobsters

Drop 1 lobster, head first, into a large pot of boiling water. Cover and cook for 3 minutes (lobster will not be fully cooked). Prepare a barbecue or grill (medium-high heat). Using tongs, transfer the lobster to a baking sheet. Return water to boil. Repeat with the second lobster. Transfer 1 lobster, shell side down, to a work surface. Place the tip of large knife into the centre of the lobster. Cut lengthwise in half from the centre to the end of the head (knife may not cut through shell) then cut in half from the centre to the end of the tail. Use poultry shears to cut through the shell. Crack the claws. Repeat with the second lobster.

Keeping lobster halves meat side up, brush shells with olive oil. Place halves, meat side up, on a barbecue. If grilling, brush meat with olive oil; sprinkle with salt and pepper. Cook until just opaque in thickest portion of tail, 7 to 9 minutes. Slice off rounds of Café de Paris butter and place over the meat and just allow to melt a little. Serve with a nice tossed salad and fresh, new potatoes.

Dorset Fishing Ports

The Jurassic Coast, for which Dorset is so famous, is not just home to a natural World Heritage Site but also to a number of attractive and lively fishing ports.

Lyme Regis, West Bay, Portland, Weymouth, Swanage, Poole and Christchurch all have commercial fish landing facilities, with a number of smaller artisan operators operating from Charmouth, Seatown, Chiswell, Lulworth and Kimmeridge.

Lyme Regis, with its famous Cobb, is renowned for the part it played in the blockbusting film 'The French Lieutenant's Woman' but it is also home to a small number of mainly owner-operated boats, which attract groups of fascinated visitors when the catches are being landed.

West Bay, with its newly refurbished harbour entrance and slipway offers both commercial and leisure fishermen the last safe haven before they tackle the massive Chesil Beach and Lyme Bay run to Portland Bill, which has a notorious tidal race.

Weymouth's 17th century harbour is a hive of marine activity and the fishing fleet competes for space with visiting yachts and other leisure users, creating a stunning visual and audio experience. As well as being home to the annual Dorset Seafood Festival, the quayside here is packed with ships' chandlers, pubs, restaurants, shops and an excellent fishmonger. Neighbouring Portland Harbour benefits from huge breakwaters: created to protect a Royal Navy long since gone, it's now a perfect base for fishermen to operate from.

Swanage, with its landing jetty is a summer venue for a number of small commercial fishermen whose main catches comprise of crabs, lobsters, cuttlefish and whelks.

Poole Harbour offers its commercial fishing fleet access to the English Channel and the Jurassic Coast. With Europe's largest natural harbour on the doorstep, the local fleet also has the opportunity to harvest seafood from within the harbour itself.

Christchurch Harbour has an inshore commercial fishing fleet based at Mudeford Quay that carries out day trips within Christchurch and Poole bays.

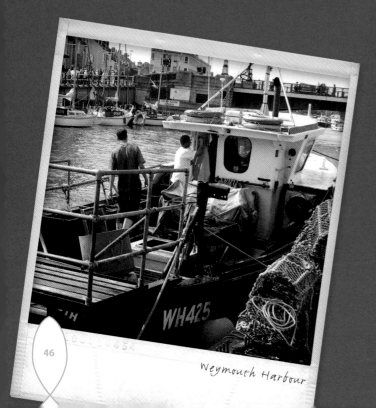

Weymouth Harbour

Lyme Regis

47

Dorset Fisheries

There are currently (2011) 216 registered commercial fishing vessels in Dorset. 80% of vessel owners are full time fishermen and with most vessels employing a crew, the industry directly employs an estimated 400 people. Alongside this the Sea Fish Industry Authority estimates that for every person at sea five are employed on land in businesses such as boatyards, marine engineers, chandlers and food outlets etc.

In addition there are over 60 charter (recreational angling and diving) vessels operating in Dorset and there is also a vibrant recreational sea angling community which has been estimated to bring income into Weymouth worth £2 million per year.

Fishing off Dorset targets a large variety of species, and many of the boats are adapted to carry a range of different types of fishing gear. The main catches for Dorset are:

Crabs & Lobster - caught in pots, these are the primary catch for many of the boats in the area. Spider Crab and Brown (Edible) Crab represent the bulk of the catch, most of which is exported to France and Spain. Lobsters are higher value but caught in smaller numbers, with more of the catch sold within the UK.

Fin-fish - the main species caught include Bass, Cod, Pollack and flat fish such as Plaice and Sole. The main catch methods are gill netting and lines. There are now only a handful of trawlers which use nets that run over the seabed targeting bottom dwelling fish.

Shellfisheries include scallops which are dredged by a small number of local boats, 'nomadic' fishers or are hand-picked by commercial divers. There is also a very significant fishery for whelks and cuttlefish, which are caught in purpose-built pots. Shellfish are particularly important within Poole Harbour, where a Fishery Order exists. The Southern IFCA leases out approximately 460 acres to allow shellfish farmers to cultivate oysters, mussels and clams. Other private shellfish beds which are cultivated commercially include the Oyster beds in the Fleet Lagoon, rope mussels in Portland Harbour and the Crown Estate has recently given the go ahead for 3 pilot lease mussel farms in the north west area of Lyme Bay. Rope culture mussel farming is generally considered one of the most environmentally sustainable ways of providing food. The Lyme Bay mussel farm covers 18km2.

Dorset Fish Species

There are over 40 edible species of fish and shellfish in Dorset waters. The table below gives the name followed by its minimum landing size. The * next to the species indicates if it is enforced by a byelaw. There are closed seasons within the district which help to conserve stocks.

Fish species	Minimum landing size cm	Fish species	Minimum landing size cm
Bass	36.0	Mackerel	20.0
* Black Seabream	23.0	Megrim	20.0
* Brill	30.0	* Mullet (Grey)	30.0
* Clams (Mercenaria mercenaria)	6.3	* Mussel	5.0
Clams (Ruditapes philippinarum)	3.5	* Oyster	7.0
Clams (Venus verrucosa)	4.0	Plaice	27.0
Clams (Ruditapes decussatus)	4.0	Pollack	30.0
* Cockle	2.38	* Queen Scallop	4.0
Cod	35.0	* Razor Clam (Ensis spp)	10.0
Crab (Brown)	14.0	* Red Mullet	15.0
Crab (Spider)	12.0 (female) 13.0 (male)	* Saithe	35.0
Crab (Velvet)	6.5	* Scad (Horse Mackerel)	15.0
* Conger Eel	58.0	* Scallop	10.0 (VII d 11.0)
Crawfish	9.5	* Shad	30.0
* Dab	23.0	* Skate (whole)	40.0
* Flounder	27.0	* Skate (wing)	20.0
Haddock	30.0	* Sole	24.0
Hake	27.0	* Surf Clam	2.5
Herring	20.0	* Turbot	30.0
* Lemon Sole	25.0	* Whelk	4.5
Ling	63.0	* Whiting	27.0
Lobster	8.7 (Carapace)	* Witch Flounder	28.0

Fishermen

The seas around our coast have provided a rich harvest for our fishing industry for generations.

During the early 1960s the fishing industry changed from a local cottage industry to a larger commercial industry. This has, over time, had an enormous effect on the fish stocks in our seas and the increase in fishing effort has undoubtedly had an impact on the marine environment.

Fishing from small ports along the south coast has always been a way of life. Sons followed fathers and grandfathers for generations; but this is rarely the case today.

So how else has the local fishing scene changed?

When I was a boy the local vessels were powered by sail, and trawling was governed by the way that the wind was blowing. In the 1940s engines were installed, which meant that a great deal more activity was possible. Nets were made of cotton and were prone to rot if not dried thoroughly. These were followed by nylon twine nets and later by monofilament.

The major changes have been to the regulations, initially coming from the UK government and later from the European Union. Long gone are the days when there were no fish quotas. Fish that were caught undersized and alive were once returned to the sea and those that were dead were used to feed the fishermen's relatively large families. The present regulations, which demand that tons of fish are returned dead to the sea as the quota has been exceeded, are beyond belief!

In recent years there has been increasing pressure from others to protect different sea creatures and marine habitats. Inshore commercial fishermen are concerned that the proposed Marine Conservation Zones will further affect the industry. The same families have fished some areas of the Purbeck coast for almost two centuries and despite the improvement in equipment, crab and lobster stocks remain steady and in some cases have improved because the fishermen have looked after their own environment.

Markets have changed too: much of the local catch in our area is shipped abroad. If only it was used locally, as is the case in many continental tourist resorts.

Sadly, with regulations increasing, the price of fuel and, despite the high retail prices, the relatively low return that local fishermen receive for their efforts, many are questioning the future of the small boat fleets. A 'way of life' is great but it does not pay the bills! ''

Ray Knight

Ray Knight

President, Poole & District Fishermen's Association

Sustainability

Commercial fishing remains an important local industry in Dorset and the challenge is to ensure that a prosperous, sustainable fishing industry continues into the future. A sustainable fishery is not just about having healthy fish populations. Methods used should maintain the balance of target species without adversely impacting other species or the environment on which they depend. There are many different methods of fishing and some, such as bottom trawling or dredging, can be more destructive to the marine environment if carried out in the wrong place. Methods such as pair trawling, which involves a large net being towed between two boats, can catch other marine creatures such as dolphins. In Dorset, pair trawling is not allowed within 6 miles of the coast. Less impacting fishing practices generally use static gear such as lobster or crab pots while some of the best examples of sustainably caught fish are line-caught mackerel and sea bass, farmed mussels and oysters and hand-picked scallops. The Southern Inshore Fisheries and Conservation Authority (Southern IFCA) who are responsible for managing the inshore fishery in Dorset, enforce the EU, National and Byelaw minimum sizes for the most commonly caught species.

By-catch is the term given to the accidental capture of 'non-target' species. It includes any marketable species caught unintentionally but also is made up of discards. Discards are the portion of a catch of fish which is returned, often dead or dying, to the sea. These fish are often unmarketable species; individuals which are below the minimum landing sizes or species which fishermen are not allowed to land due to EU quota restrictions. Trawls and purse-seine nets have high levels of by-catch.

Continues on page 57

Continued from page 54

In the UK, the demand for fish and shellfish from the public has increased over the years as the health benefits of consuming fish have been publicised and promoted, and as fish products have become more widely available in supermarkets.   The increase in more sophisticated technologies, such as sonar and radar-based fish sensors, has allowed the fishing industry to keep up with this demand, but is also putting more pressure on fish populations, with fish being easier to find and to catch. Many smaller day fishing boats have been replaced by large industrial vessels that can spend weeks out at sea. However, the Southern IFCA has a byelaw restricting the size of vessel that can fish off the coast of Dorset, Hampshire and the Isle of Wight to 12 metres.

In Dorset, there is a diverse fishery with many local fishermen still using small day fishing boats. Having a variety of fish to catch means that fishermen can land many different species, which can help keep the fish stocks in balance and reduce over fishing of one particular type of fish.

Fish are generally very mobile, and many have annual migrations. Crustacea, particularly crabs, also move considerable distances on and offshore as the seasons change. Dorset's coastal waters provide important spawning and nursery areas for a range of different marine species. Fish larvae produced here support the future of the fishery in Dorset and beyond.

Fishermen's Mission

We often take for granted the boats and fishermen that bring the wonderful bounty to our shores. However, fishing remains the most dangerous peacetime occupation and there is increasing pressure on the under 10-metre fleet, such as those in Dorset, just to make their boats pay and to keep fishing communities alive. All down the south west coast fishing communities are disappearing, and once they are gone they will be gone forever. A Dorset quayside without its fishing boats would not only be a sadder place but also have deep social and economic consequences for the wider community.

Over 13,000 men and women work in the UK's toughest occupation, deep sea fishing. At sea, they face death and injury on a daily basis. On land, many face insecurity and debt. And life for the 50,000 retired fishermen and their dependants is no better, with debt, inadequate pensions and scant savings meaning no respite from hardship once the fishing is over.

The Fishermen's Mission fights poverty and despair in our fishing communities by providing emergency and welfare support to fishermen and their families 24 hours a day, 7 days a week, 365 days a year.

www.fishermensmission.org.uk

£1.00 from every cook book sold will be donated to the Fishermen's Mission.

Jos Standerwick at the Dorset Seafood Festival in aid of the Fishermen's Mission

FISHERMEN'S MISSION

IF YOU HAVE ANY SPARE CHANGE PLEASE **WANG IT IN THE WELLY**

WWW.PERRYSRESTAURANT.CO.UK PERRY'S

FRIDGE MAGNETS
CRABS - £2·00
SQUID - £2·00
LOBSTERS - £2·00
OR
3 for £5·00

FRIDGE MAGNETS

£5.00
2011 Edition

ISBN 978-0-9569454-0-2

9 780956 945402 >